Crabapples

Horses

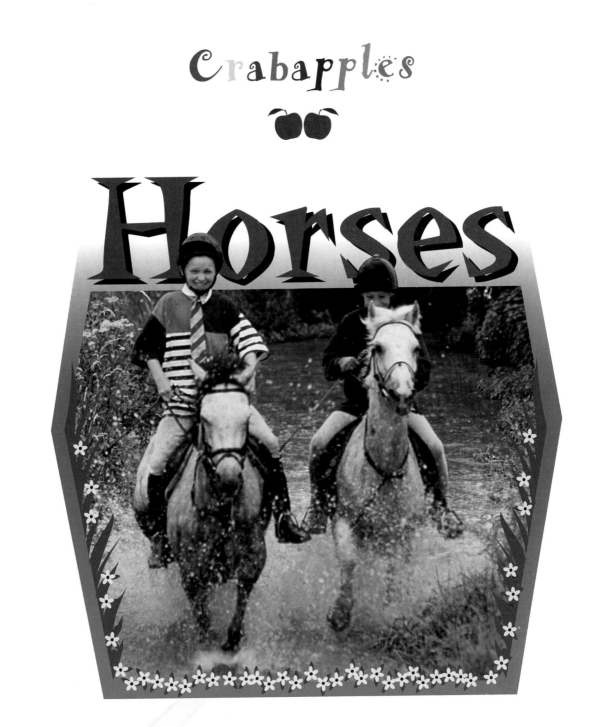

Tammy Everts & Bobbie Kalman

🌳 Crabtree Publishing Con

Crabapples

created by Bobbie Kalman

For Tiffany and Tyler

Editor-in-Chief
Bobbie Kalman

Writing team
Tammy Everts
Bobbie Kalman

Managing editor
Lynda Hale

Editors
Petrina Gentile
Niki Walker
Greg Nickles

Computer design
Lynda Hale

Photographs
Bob Langrish

Illustrations
Jeannette McNaughton-Julich: pages 8-9, 12-13
Tammy Everts: pages 7, 26, 27

Color separations and film
Dot 'n Line Image Inc.

Printer
Worzalla Publishing Company

Crabtree Publishing Company

350 Fifth Avenue
Suite 3308
New York
N.Y. 10118

360 York Road, RR 4,
Niagara-on-the-Lake,
Ontario, Canada
L0S 1J0

73 Lime Walk
Headington
Oxford OX3 7AD
United Kingdom

Cataloging in Publication Data
Everts, Tammy, 1970-
    Horses

(Crabapples)
Includes index.

ISBN 0-86505-623-4 (library bound)   ISBN 0-86505-723-0 (pbk.)
This book describes many aspects of horses, including riding, care, grooming, and descriptions of a variety of breeds.

1. Horses - Juvenile literature. I. Kalman, Bobbie, 1947-   .
II. Title. III. Series: Kalman, Bobbie, 1947-   . Crabapples.

SF302.E84 1995   j636.1   LC 95-37903
                                                        CIP

What is in this book?

All about horses

Horses are **mammals**. Mammals are **warm-blooded**. Their bodies have hair or fur. A baby mammal drinks its mother's milk.

A male horse is called a **stallion**, and a female horse is a **mare**. Baby horses are **foals**. Wild horses live in groups called **herds**. A stallion, a few mares, and their foals make up a herd. The members of the herd protect one another from danger.

A horse's body

Horses have excellent senses for detecting enemies and long, strong legs for running away from them. Although they no longer have natural enemies, horses were once hunted by bears, wild cats, and other **predators**.

rump

A long tail is useful for flicking away flies and mosquitoes.

The **hoof** is actually a toe. Horses have only one toe on each foot.

mane

muzzle

elbow

knee

Horses hear very well. Their large ears can move around and "catch" sounds.

The eyes are set high on both sides of the head, allowing the horse to see in different directions.

An adult horse has 40 teeth. As the horse ages, its teeth wear down and turn brown. A person can tell a horse's age by looking at its teeth.

A horse's height is measured in **hands**. One hand equals ten centimeters (four inches). The horse is measured from its hooves to the top of its shoulders.

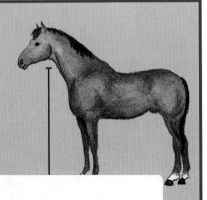

Colors and marks

Many horse colors have special names. The marks on a horse's face and legs help people identify the different horses in a herd.

star

snip

blaze

stripe

brown

palomino

gray

dapple-gray

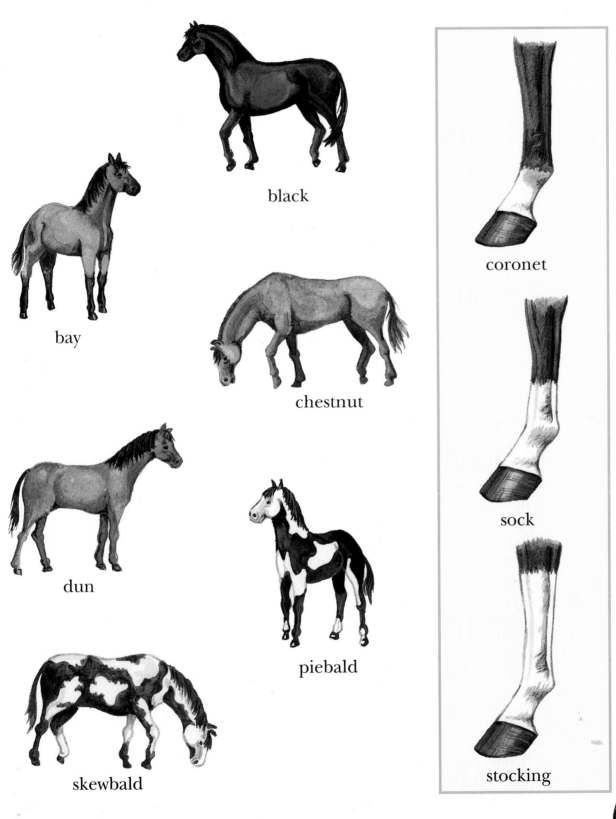

black

bay

chestnut

dun

piebald

skewbald

coronet

sock

stocking

9

Foals

Horses mate in the springtime, and foals are born a year later. Usually only one foal is born at a time. A male foal is called a **colt**. A female is a **filly**.

After the foal is born, its mother licks it clean. The foal tries to stand on its thin, wobbly legs. Within an hour, it takes shaky steps and drinks its first milk, called **colostrum**. The colostrum contains special vitamins that help protect the foal against diseases.

When it is about a month old, the foal begins to graze on shoots of grass. It will still suckle its mother's milk for up to a year.

The horse family tree

Horses belong to the same large family as zebras and asses. There are three species of zebras, two species of asses, and one species of horse. Horses are divided into 200 different **breeds**. Ponies are small horses. Donkeys are asses that have been tamed.

Horse

Asses

Asiatic ass

African ass

The ancestor of the horse is the **hyracotherium**, which lived 55 million years ago. It had four toes on each foot and was the size of a large rabbit.

Zebras

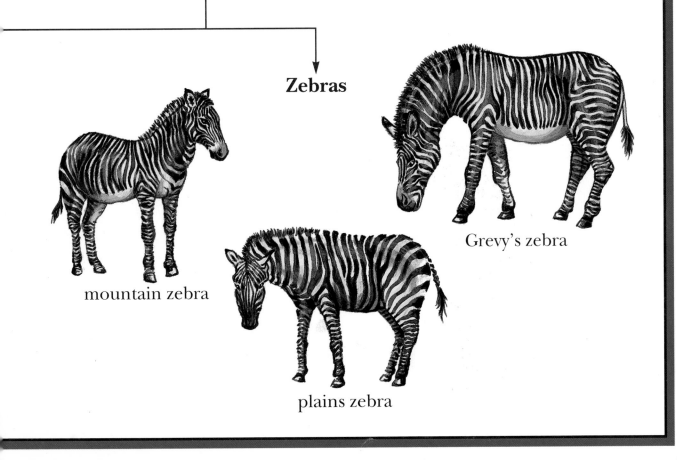

mountain zebra

plains zebra

Grevy's zebra

Shetland pony

The Shetland pony is named after its
first home—the stormy Shetland Islands
off the coast of Scotland. The Shetland
pony is one of the smallest breeds of
horse, but it is very strong and tough.
It can pull a load twice its own weight.
A hundred years ago, Shetland ponies
pulled carts in coal mines. Today,
Shetland ponies are popular pets
for young children.

Clydesdale

The Clydesdale is one of the largest and strongest horses. It has big bones and bulky muscles. Farmers use Clydesdales to pull heavy plows, sleds, and wagons. It is easy to identify a Clydesdale by the long hair around its hooves. This long hair is called **feathering**, or **feathers**.

Plains horses

Hundreds of years ago, the Native peoples of North America tamed the horses of the plains. Appaloosas and pintos were favorite horses because they were small, strong, and brave. They were useful for hunting bison.

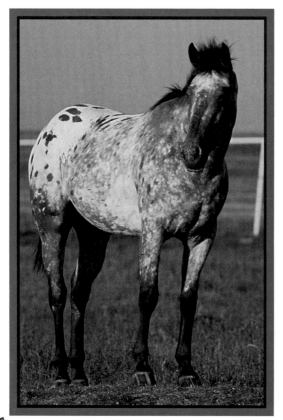

The pinto and appaloosa have similar builds, but it is easy to tell them apart. A pinto's spots look like large splotches of paint, which is why pintos are sometimes called "paints."

An appaloosa has many small spots. Over fifty years ago, appaloosas were in danger of dying out. Many horse-lovers worked together to keep this horse breed alive. Today, the appaloosa is a popular breed.

Arabian

One of the world's oldest horse breeds is the Arabian. All modern racehorses are descendants of Arabians that lived and raced over a thousand years ago.

Arabians are small, powerful horses with long legs and arched necks. They are admired for their speed, grace, and high spirits.

Arabians are beautiful, but they are hard to handle. They are nervous animals that need skillful trainers.

Morgan

The calm, courageous Morgan horse was popular in the United States hundreds of years ago. Early settlers liked the Morgan because it could carry a rider over rough roads for hours without tiring. Today, this sturdy breed makes an excellent riding horse and a loyal companion. Morgans are often used by mounted police officers.

Lipizzan

The dazzling white Lipizzans of Austria have performed their graceful, ballet-like dance for hundreds of years. These beautiful horses were first trained as war horses, but today they perform for huge audiences. They receive their dance training at a special school called the Spanish Riding School.

Only stallions are trained at the Spanish Riding School. They are sent to the school when they are four years old and are gently encouraged to perform movements that come naturally to them. It takes many years of patient training before the stallions are ready to perform their dance for an audience.

Wild horses

Przewalski's horse, shown below, is the only true wild horse alive today. Przewalski's horse has never been tamed, but hundreds live in zoos.

Many other horses are called "wild." They are descended from tame horses that escaped or were released into the wild. These "wild" horses live in many parts of the world.

The white Camargue pony on the opposite page lives in the marshes of France. Farmers use tame Camargues to help round up cattle.

Herds of mustangs roam the American plains. The word mustang means "ownerless."

Hundreds of ponies live on the island of Assateague, off the eastern coast of the United States. Assateague has been turned into a wildlife refuge.

Horses at work

People began to tame horses over 4,000 years ago. Long before cars and trucks were invented, horses pulled carts and fought in wars. Horses still have many jobs. They do heavy work, round up herds of animals, and entertain people.

Some horses work on farms. They pull plows, carts, and heavy wagons. Well-trained ranch horses help cowboys and cowgirls herd cattle and sheep. They also herd other horses.

Many years ago, officers with the Royal Canadian Mounted Police rode horses. Today, they ride horses only on special occasions when they perform an event called the Musical Ride.

A **mane comb** frees the mane and tail of snarls.

A **dandy brush** removes dried mud from the coat.

Horse care

A horse must be fed hay, oats, grain, and grass to stay healthy. To keep a horse beautiful, it is important to care for its coat, mane, and tail. This kind of care is called **grooming**. Grooming is important because dirt and dried mud under the saddle can irritate the horse's skin. Horse grooming takes a lot of time and requires special tools.

A **body brush** cleans the coat and smooths the mane and tail.

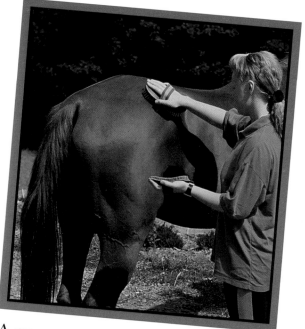

A **curry comb**, held in one hand, cleans the brush.

Horses wear shoes to protect their hooves from painful cracks and breaks. The shoes are attached to the hooves with nails, but do not worry—having shoes put on does not hurt. This work is done by a skilled person called a **farrier**.

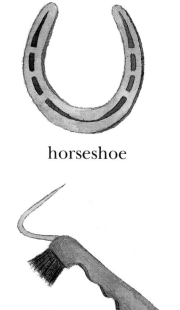

horseshoe

There are other ways to protect a horse's hooves. A **hoof pick** removes sharp stones that could crack the hoof. A coat of **hoof oil** cleans and strengthens the hooves and makes them shine.

hoof pick

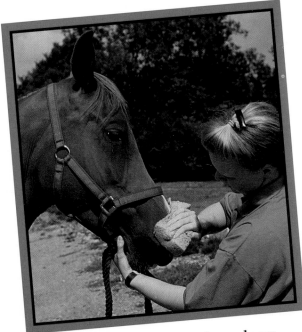

A damp sponge is used to clean the eyes, mouth, and nose.

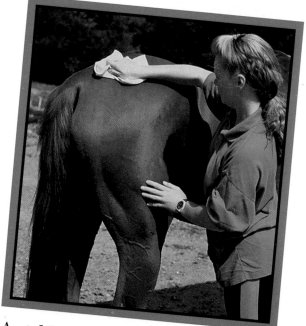

A **stable rubber** is used to polish the coat and make it shine.

Saddle up

Long ago, people sat on blankets while riding horses. Today, horses wear **saddles** and **bridles**. This equipment, called **tack**, makes the ride safer and more comfortable for the rider and horse.

Saddle

horn

cantle

seat

saddle lining

girth strap

lace strings

fender

stirrup

Bridle

headpiece

browband

cheekpiece

noseband

throatlatch

reins

bit

Giddy-up!

To get on, or **mount**, the horse, the rider puts one foot in a stirrup and lifts the other leg over the saddle. When both feet are securely in the stirrups, the rider is ready to go. Horses move at different paces, called **gaits**. The slowest gait is the **walk**. The fastest is the **gallop**.

The **walk** is a slow gait.

A **trot** is a fast walk.

Jumping is more difficult than it looks. As the horse approaches the fence, or **hurdle**, the rider presses with his or her knees to stay seated. The rider leans over the horse's neck and holds on tightly to the reins.

Horses and riders often jump in shows. A jumping race, called a **steeplechase**, is a fast, challenging event.

A **canter** is a slow run.

A **gallop** is a fast run.

Words to know

breed A variety of a species of animal

colostrum The first milk a foal drinks from its mother's body

colt A young male horse

farrier A person who equips horses with shoes

feathers The long hair around some horses' hooves

filly A young female horse

foal A young horse

gait The pace at which a horse moves

groom To clean and brush an animal's coat

hand A unit used for measuring a horse's height

herd A large group of horses

hurdle A fencelike obstacle over which a horse jumps

mammal A class of warm-blooded animals with backbones

mare An adult female horse

mount To get onto a horse's back

predator An animal that hunts and eats other animals

stallion An adult male horse

steeplechase A race in which horses jump over several hurdles

tack The equipment needed to ride a horse

warm-blooded Describes having a body temperature that stays the same no matter how warm or cold the environment is

Index

1 2 3 4 5 6 7 8 9 0 Printed in the U.S.A. 4 3 2 1 0 9 8 7 6 5

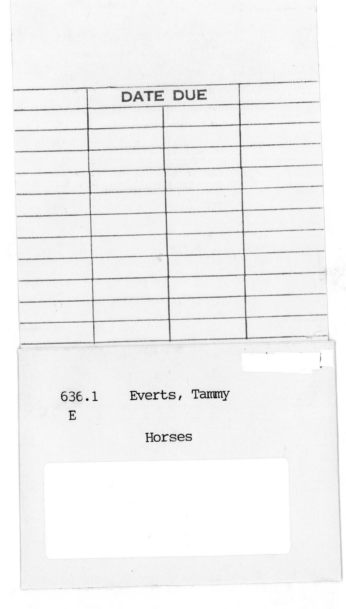

DATE DUE